ETH ER EUM

THE QUIET EVOLUTION

How does cryptocurrency transform the world

CRYPTO
R=VOLUTION

SOMMAIRE

Introduction

In the vast universe of cryptocurrencies and blockchain technology, one name stands out with a promise of innovation and transformation: Ethereum. More than just a digital currency, Ethereum represents a comprehensive platform that offers a new horizon of opportunities and challenges, reshaping our understanding of decentralized currencies.

From the dark days of the internet's underground, where cryptocurrencies were barely understood, if not outright dismissed, to today, where they dominate headlines in the financial world, the world has witnessed the birth and growth of numerous blockchain initiatives. However, Ethereum sets itself apart with its unique approach, focused not only on a cryptocurrency, Ether, but also on a platform that enables the creation and management of smart contracts and decentralized applications.

Ethereum's vision, championed by its creator, Vitalik Buterin, was to create a decentralized «world computer» where applications could run without any central point of failure, providing transparency, security, and, most importantly, true decentralization. This grand vision has already begun to materialize in various domains, from financial services to art, gaming, and real estate.

But what makes Ethereum so special? Is it just another «cryptocurrency,» or is it the logical next step in the evolution of blockchain technology? In this book, we will delve deep into the world of Ethereum, exploring its history, technology, applications, and its potential to reshape the world as we know it. We will also examine the challenges Ethereum faces and how it may evolve in the future.

Whether you are a curious newcomer to the world of cryptocurrencies, a developer seeking to understand the power of smart contracts, or an investor trying to grasp the nuances of decentralized finance, this book aims to guide you through the fascinating saga of Ethereum.

1

Ethereum's History

ORIGINS: WHO IS VITALIK BUTERIN AND WHAT WAS HIS VISION?

Vitalik Buterin: The Visionary Prodigy of Ethereum

In the dynamic world of blockchain and cryptocurrencies, certain individuals have emerged as leaders, innovators, and true pioneers. Vitalik Buterin is undoubtedly one of these personalities, having co-founded Ethereum, the second-largest cryptocurrency by market capitalization, after Bitcoin. But who is Vitalik, and what vision drove him to create Ethereum?

A Computer Prodigy

Born in 1994 in Kolomna, Russia, Vitalik Buterin moved to Canada with his family at a young age. From his childhood, he demonstrated exceptional aptitude for mathematics and logic. In school, he was already recognized for his math skills, winning medals in scholastic competitions. His love for computer science and decentralized systems began when he discovered Bitcoin in 2011. Fascinated by this new technology, he started writing articles about Bitcoin for a blog, earning his first Bitcoins.

From a Writer to an Innovator

Vitalik's interest wasn't limited to Bitcoin as a currency. He was particularly captivated by the possibilities offered by the underlying blockchain technology. In 2012, he co-founded the «Bitcoin Magazine,» where he wrote numerous articles on various aspects of cryptocurrencies. However, while working on Bitcoin, he identified limitations in its design. Although Bitcoin was a decentralized currency, Vitalik envisioned a platform where anyone could create decentralized applications, not just monetary transactions. It was this vision that led to the birth of Ethereum.

Ethereum: A Bold Vision

Vitalik envisioned a new blockchain that would go beyond what Bitcoin offered. Instead of just a currency, he saw a platform. A platform where anyone could write scripts, called «smart contracts,» that would automatically execute under certain conditions. This was a revolutionary idea because it would decentralize any digital service, whether it was voting systems, real estate, financial services, or art.

In 2013, he published a whitepaper describing this vision. Instead of extending Bitcoin's functionality, he proposed creating an entirely separate blockchain with a complete programming language. This proposal was well-received by the community, and with the help of other co-founders, the Ethereum project was launched.

In Conclusion

Vitalik Buterin's story is that of a young prodigy who became one of the most influential figures in the blockchain world. His vision for Ethereum has been a game-changer, opening up a world of possibilities for decentralized applications. Today, thanks to his leadership and determination, Ethereum continues to be at the forefront of innovation, constantly redefining the boundaries of what is possible with blockchain technology.

THE BIRTH OF ETHEREUM: THE ICO AND THE DAWNING OF A NEW ERA

The genesis of Ethereum is an essential chapter in the history of cryptocurrencies.

However, to fully grasp this birth, one must delve into the complex and innovative mechanisms through which it materialized, notably the Initial Coin Offering (ICO).

So, how did Ethereum transition from the idea of a young visionary to a tangible reality, and what role did the ICO play in all of this? Join me on this historical journey.

An Idea in Search of Funding

After unveiling his vision of Ethereum to the world through a whitepaper in 2013, Vitalik Buterin and his team of co-founders faced a significant challenge: how to finance such an ambitious project? At that time, the world of cryptocurrencies was still largely uncharted territory, and most people were skeptical about the feasibility and viability of innovative ideas like Ethereum.

This is where the concept of an ICO, or Initial Coin Offering, came into play. Inspired by the Initial Public Offerings (IPOs) in the world of stocks, an ICO is a way for startups to raise funds by pre-selling tokens that will have utility in their future project. These tokens are often likened to shares, although they generally do not confer ownership or voting rights.

Ethereum's ICO: A Record-Breaking Fundraising

In 2014, Ethereum launched its ICO, offering investors the opportunity to purchase «Ethers» (ETH), the fuel that would power its platform. To provide some perspective, the price of one Ether during this ICO was approximately $0.30. The world responded with resounding enthusiasm.

In just 42 days, Ethereum had raised over $18 million, making it the largest cryptocurrency fundraising ever at that time. This ICO not only provided the necessary funds to develop the platform but also served as validation of the Ethereum concept. Thousands of investors worldwide believed in Vitalik's vision and his team.

The Early Post-ICO Days

Following a successful ICO, the pressure on the Ethereum team was immense. They had to turn their vision into a functional reality. For nearly a year, the team worked tirelessly to develop, test, and refine the platform. In July 2015, the first version of Ethereum, called «Frontier,» was launched.

It was a pivotal moment. Developers from around the world began creating applications on Ethereum, experimenting with smart contracts, and exploring the limitless possibilities offered by the platform. Of course, there were challenges and issues to overcome, but the growing Ethereum community rallied together to tackle them.

Conclusion

The birth of Ethereum is a story of innovation, perseverance, and community. The ICO not only enabled the realization of the vision but also laid the foundation for a vibrant ecosystem that would support and further develop the platform in the years to come. Looking back, these early days were pivotal, setting the first stone of a technological monument that would transform our perception and utilization of blockchain.

THE DAO AND THE FORK:
ETHEREUM AND ETHEREUM CLASSIC

The DAO, the Fork, and the Ethereum Duality: From Unification to Split

The world of cryptocurrencies is brimming with fascinating stories, and the episode of the DAO (Decentralized Autonomous Organization) in Ethereum's history is undoubtedly one of the most intriguing. This incident not only highlighted the risks and challenges associated with smart contracts and decentralization but also led to a fracture in the Ethereum community, giving rise to two distinct chains: Ethereum (ETH) and Ethereum Classic (ETC). Let's dive together into this tumultuous episode.

The DAO: The Decentralized Utopia

The DAO was a decentralized investment fund built on the Ethereum platform. Its goal was simple: to allow anyone to submit projects and receive funding, without intermediaries, purely based on the votes of DAO token holders. In theory, this seemed to be the perfect embodiment of decentralization: a self-governing organization, led by a community, without a centralized structure.

In 2016, the DAO conducted an impressive fundraising, amassing the equivalent of $150 million in Ether. But the euphoria was short-lived.

The Vulnerability and Attack

Shortly after its creation, researchers and developers began to report potential vulnerabilities in the DAO's code. Unfortunately, before corrective measures could be put in place, an individual or group (who remains unknown) exploited one of these vulnerabilities. The attacker siphoned off one-third of the DAO's funds, approximately $50 million at the time.

The attack sent shockwaves through the community. Not only were large sums of money at stake, but the very integrity of Ethereum was called into question. The platform designed to revolutionize decentralized contracts and organizations had been compromised.

The Fork Decision: A Divided Community

Faced with this crisis, the Ethereum community found itself in a moral and technical dilemma. Should they intervene and «rollback» the transaction to recover the funds, risking the ideology of immutability and decentralization? Or should they accept the loss and continue, preserving the chain's integrity?

After many debates, a decision was made: a «hard fork» would be executed. This technical intervention would create a new chain where the DAO's funds would be returned to their original owners. However, not everyone agreed with this decision. Some of the community believed that the immutability of the blockchain should not be compromised, no matter the circumstances.

This is how Ethereum Classic (ETC) was born. Those who did not accept the hard fork and wanted to maintain the original chain continued on this new chain, defending the idea that «code is law,» meaning that once deployed, the code must remain immutable.

In Conclusion

The DAO incident and the subsequent split are pivotal moments in Ethereum's history. They serve as a reminder of the challenges, both technical and ethical, associated with decentralization and governance. Today, Ethereum and Ethereum Classic coexist, each with its own vision and community. This story is a testament to the complexity, passion, and innovation that drive the world of cryptocurrencies.

2

Understanding the Basics

WHAT IS ETHEREUM'S BLOCKCHAIN?

Ethereum's Blockchain: The Web of Infinite Possibilities

When we talk about blockchain, many immediately think of Bitcoin, the revolutionary cryptocurrency that rocked the financial world. However, while Bitcoin is the revered ancestor of cryptocurrencies, Ethereum is the polymath prodigy, bringing an entirely new dimension to the blockchain universe. So, what makes Ethereum's blockchain so special? Hold on tight, we're about to dive into the heart of this digital web.

What is a Blockchain?

To understand the uniqueness of Ethereum's blockchain, it's essential to first grasp the fundamentals of what a basic blockchain is. Imagine a ledger accessible to everyone, where each transaction is recorded sequentially. Each page of this ledger is a «block,» and each block is linked to the previous one through cryptography, forming a «chain.» This ledger is copied thousands of times worldwide, ensuring its security and transparency.

Ethereum: Beyond Just Currency

If Bitcoin introduced the concept of blockchain as a ledger for monetary transactions, Ethereum expanded this vision to include any form of programmable information or operation. The idea behind Ethereum was to create a universal and decentralized platform on which any application could be built. Rather than merely being a «ledger» for transactions, Ethereum's blockchain is more like a «world computer.»

Smart Contracts: Ethereum's Brain

At the core of Ethereum's value proposition are «smart contracts.» These self-executing pieces of code are deployed on the blockchain and automatically execute when certain conditions are met. For example, a smart contract can be programmed to release funds when two parties have fulfilled their respective obligations. It's like an automated agent, except it's unstoppable, transparent, and free from external interference.

Ether: Ethereum's Fuel

While Bitcoin has «bitcoin» as its currency, Ethereum has «Ether» (ETH). However, Ether is not just a currency. It serves as the «fuel» to execute operations on Ethereum's blockchain. Every action, whether it's sending tokens, running a smart contract, or launching an application, requires a certain amount of Ether as «gas» fees. This ensures network efficiency because users must weigh the necessity of their actions against their cost.

Decentralization and Innovation

One of Ethereum's key advantages is its decentralized nature. Instead of being stored on a centralized server, information on Ethereum is distributed across thousands of nodes worldwide. This makes it resistant to censorship, fraud, and single points of failure. Moreover, this decentralization has given rise to an ecosystem of innovators, developers, and entrepreneurs working together to create decentralized applications (dApps) spanning from financial markets to gaming and beyond.

In Conclusion

Ethereum's blockchain, with its flexibility, resilience, and thriving ecosystem, is more than just a technology. It's a vision of a decentralized internet, where individuals regain control of their data and interact directly with each other without intermediaries. While the future remains uncertain, one thing is clear: Ethereum has already redefined what we think is possible in the digital world.

ETHER VS. ETHEREUM: DISTINGUISHING THE PLATFORM FROM ITSNATIVE CURRENCY

Ether vs. Ethereum: A Subtle Dance between a World Computer and its Fuel

When delving into the fascinating world of cryptocurrencies, it's easy to get lost in a sea of technical terms and innovative concepts. Among these terms, two words, often used interchangeably but profoundly distinct, stand out: Ethereum and Ether. To grasp the landscape of Ethereum as a whole, it's essential to distinguish these two elements and recognize their respective roles. So, what sets Ethereum apart from Ether? And why is this distinction so crucial?

Ethereum: The World Computer

A BOLD VISION: At the core of the Ethereum project lies a revolutionary ambition: to create a decentralized world computer. This is not a computer in the traditional sense, with a screen, keyboard, and mouse. No, it's a platform, an infrastructure that spans the globe across thousands of machines, working together to execute code and applications.

THE INFRASTRUCTURE: Therefore, Ethereum is this infrastructure, this foundation upon which various applications are built. Just as the Internet serves as the foundation for websites like Google or Facebook, Ethereum serves as the basis for a multitude of decentralized applications (dApps).

SMART CONTRACTS: The magic of Ethereum lies in its ability to execute «smart contracts.» Imagine contracts that automatically execute, without intermediaries, as soon as their predefined conditions are met. It's as if you had a notary, a banker, and a lawyer rolled into one entity, working 24/7 without ever making a mistake.

Ether: Ethereum's Fuel

MORE THAN JUST CURRENCY: When most people hear about cryptocurrency, they think of digital currency used to purchase goods and services. This is where Ether comes into play. But Ether is much more than just a currency. It's the fuel that powers the Ethereum network.

GAS FEES: Every action on Ethereum, whether it's sending Ether to a friend, launching an application, or executing a smart contract, comes with a cost. This cost, measured in «gas,» is paid in Ether. This ensures that users are judicious in their actions, preventing network congestion.

MEANS AND REWARD: Ether also serves as a reward for «miners,» individuals who lend their computer's computing power to verify and validate transactions on Ethereum. By rewarding miners with Ether, the platform incentivizes them to continue their work, ensuring the security and efficiency of the network.

Why This Distinction is Crucial?

Understanding the difference between Ethereum and Ether is essential for several reasons. Firstly, it provides a clear view of how the ecosystem operates: Ethereum as the stage, and Ether as the spotlight illuminating it. Secondly, it helps investors and users make informed decisions, whether it's investing in Ether as an asset or using Ethereum as a development platform.

In Conclusion

Ethereum and Ether are two sides of the same coin, each playing a unique role in the decentralization ballet. By clearly distinguishing the platform from its native currency, one can better appreciate the beauty and complexity of this ever-evolving world.

SMART CONTRACTS: THE HEART OF ETHEREUM

Smart Contracts: The Pulse of the Ethereum Revolution

The world of cryptocurrencies is vast, dense, and often nebulous. But if one star shines particularly bright in this space, it's the concept of «Smart Contracts.» Introduced and popularized by Ethereum, these smart contracts transform our understanding of what automated transactions, agreements, and interactions can be.

What is a Smart Contract?

Imagine an automated vending machine: you insert a coin, select a product, and the machine delivers it to you. There's no human behind this machine; everything is automated, based on the machine's predefined rules. Smart contracts work on a similar principle, but in Ethereum's digital world. A smart contract is a self-executing program with direct instructions written into its code. It's deployed on the Ethereum blockchain, and once certain predefined conditions are met, the contract executes itself, without intermediaries, in a transparent and immutable manner.

Why Are They «Smart»?

The term «smart» doesn't mean these contracts have consciousness or thinking ability. Instead, their «intelligence» lies in their ability to execute automatically, without requiring human intervention, once their predetermined conditions are satisfied. They eliminate the need for intermediaries, reducing costs, errors, and the risk of manipulation.

Benefits of Smart Contracts

TRANSPARENCY: Contract terms are visible and accessible to all parties involved.

SECURITY: Once deployed on the blockchain, the contract is encrypted and becomes immutable. It's nearly impossible to hack.

EFFICIENCY: Automated transactions and agreements save time and eliminate the usual delays associated with traditional processes.

COST SAVINGS: By removing intermediaries like lawyers or notaries, transaction costs are greatly reduced.

RELIABILITY: Automation significantly reduces the risk of human errors.

Real-World Applications

Smart contracts have an almost infinite range of applications:

REAL ESTATE: Imagine buying a house without needing a notary. The smart contract can be programmed to transfer ownership once payment is made.

VOTING SYSTEMS: Transparent and fraud-resistant elections through contracts that automatically and securely record each vote.
Supply Chain: Every step of the supply chain, from manufacturing to delivery, can be tracked, verified, and automated through smart contracts.

Some Limitations

However, smart contracts are not perfect. Since they are code-based, they are only as good (or bad) as the developers who write them. A coding error could have unfortunate consequences, as seen in the 2016 DAO incident. Furthermore, their immutable nature means that once deployed, they are difficult to change.

In Conclusion

Smart contracts are the beating heart of Ethereum, redefining the concept of transactions and interactions in a digital world. They embody the promise of a more transparent, efficient, and equitable world. While they have their share of challenges, their potential is undeniable, and their impact on society could be as significant as the advent of the internet itself.

3

Ethereum's Technology

HOW PROOF-OF-WORK OPERATES

Proof-of-Work (PoW): The Guardian of the Blockchain Temple

In the vast ecosystem of cryptocurrencies, several concepts may seem inscrutable at first glance. One of them, essential for the security and reliability of transactions, is the consensus mechanism called «Proof-of-Work» (PoW). While this term may appear obscure, it is, in fact, at the core of many cryptocurrencies, including the famous Bitcoin. Let's delve into the intricacies of this ingenious system together.

What is Proof-of-Work (PoW)?

Imagine a massive, complex puzzle that requires significant effort to solve. Once this puzzle is completed, it's easy for anyone to verify that the pieces fit together correctly. This is a simplified analogy of PoW. PoW is a mechanism that makes certain tasks difficult and resource-intensive in terms of time and resources but makes the verification of these tasks easy for others. In the context of cryptocurrencies, this «puzzle» is a complex mathematical problem that miners must solve.

Why Use Such a System?

PoW serves several purposes:

SECURITY: By demanding a substantial amount of resources and energy to solve puzzles, PoW discourages malicious attacks. A hacker would need a colossal amount of computing power to take control of the network, making it unprofitable.

FAIRNESS: PoW ensures that those who contribute to the network (miners) are rewarded for their work. The more effort a miner invests, the more likely they are to solve the puzzle and receive a reward.

INTEGRITY: Thanks to PoW, each block added to the blockchain carries proof of its authenticity. It's nearly impossible to alter a block once added, ensuring the reliability of transactions.

The Mining Process via PoW

PUZZLE SOLVING: Miners receive a list of pending transactions. They must then solve a complex mathematical problem that requires immense computational power. This problem is based on the content of the previous block, ensuring the continuity and security of the chain.

REWARD: The first miner to solve the puzzle broadcasts their solution to the network. Other miners verify this solution (which is easy and quick). If it is correct, the block is added to the blockchain, and the miner is rewarded in cryptocurrency.

ADDITION TO THE BLOCKCHAIN: Once consensus is reached, the new block is added to the chain irreversibly.

Critiques and Limitations

Although PoW is a groundbreaking invention, it has drawbacks:

ENERGY CONSUMPTION: PoW requires enormous amounts of energy. Massive mining farms, often powered by fossil fuels, have concerning environmental impacts.

CENTRALIZATION OF MINING: Over time, mining has become so competitive that only large corporations can afford the necessary infrastructure, unintentionally leading to centralization.

In Conclusion

Proof-of-Work is an essential pillar of the cryptocurrency world, ensuring security, fairness, and integrity in otherwise decentralized systems. While criticized for its disadvantages, it remains, at least for now, the foundation on which the operation of many digital currencies relies.

TRANSITIONING TO PROOF-OF-STAKE: ETHEREUM 2.0

Ethereum's Transition to Proof-of-Stake: Decrypting Ethereum 2.0

The blockchain universe is in constant evolution, with Ethereum at the forefront of this technological revolution. While the initial iteration of Ethereum relied on the Proof-of-Work (PoW) consensus mechanism, much like Bitcoin, a major transition is on the horizon: Ethereum 2.0 and its shift to Proof-of-Stake (PoS). To grasp this transition, let's dive into the world of Ethereum 2.0.

Ethereum: A Quick Retrospective

Since its inception in 2015, Ethereum has gained popularity for its ability to execute «smart contracts» on its platform. But like any technology, it faces challenges, particularly regarding scalability, security, and energy consumption.

What is Ethereum 2.0?

Ethereum 2.0, often referred to as Eth2 or Serenity, is a major upgrade to the Ethereum platform aimed at enhancing the network's speed, efficiency, and sustainability. It comprises a series of interconnected updates that will radically transform the network's operation.

Why Transition to Proof-of-Stake?

While PoW has been effective in securing blockchains, it is highly energy-intensive. Miners, in their efforts to validate transactions and create new blocks, consume a considerable amount of computational power. PoS offers a less energy-consuming alternative, where validators replace miners by «staking» a certain number of their tokens as collateral.

Phases of Ethereum 2.0

PHASE 0: Introduced the Beacon Chain in December 2020, a PoS blockchain running parallel to the main Ethereum chain, laying the groundwork for future updates.

PHASE 1: Expected in 2021, this phase will introduce shard chains, essentially small parallel blockchains. These shard chains will increase Ethereum's processing capacity, allowing the network to handle more transactions simultaneously.

PHASE 1.5: At this stage, the original Ethereum blockchain (PoW) will merge with the Beacon Chain (PoS), marking Ethereum's complete transition to PoS.

PHASE 2: This phase, still under discussion, may bring further enhancements, particularly regarding smart contracts.

Advantages and Implications of Ethereum 2.0

ENERGY EFFICIENCY: Reduced energy consumption, making the network more environmentally friendly.

ENHANCED SECURITY: With more people having the opportunity to become validators through PoS, the network becomes more decentralized and potentially more secure.

INCREASED CAPACITY: With the introduction of shard chains, Ethereum can process many more transactions, addressing congestion issues encountered in the past.

Challenges of the Transition

Despite the excitement, the shift to Ethereum 2.0 is not without risks. Massive technological migrations can encounter unforeseen bugs or vulnerabilities. Additionally, convincing the entire community to support and adopt these changes is also a challenge.

In Conclusion

Ethereum 2.0 represents the promising future of the Ethereum blockchain. This transition to PoS is a bold response to the sustainability and scalability challenges faced by many blockchains. As this upgrade continues to unfold, the cryptocurrency industry will closely follow, as the implications for the future of decentralized finance are immense.

TECHNICAL CHALLENGES: SCALABILITY, SECURITY, AND UPGRADES

Ethereum's Technical Challenges: Scalability, Security, and Upgrades

The world of cryptocurrencies and blockchains is fascinating but riddled with complex technical challenges. Ethereum, as one of the leading blockchain platforms, is not immune to these challenges. Three of the primary issues Ethereum has faced and continues to grapple with are scalability, security, and the ability to perform upgrades or updates. Let's delve into each of these aspects for a clear and detailed understanding.

Scalability: A Network Bottleneck

WHAT IS SCALABILITY?

Scalability refers to a system's ability to handle an increased workload. For Ethereum, this means processing a greater number of transactions as more users join the network.

WHY IS IT A PROBLEM?

In its early days, Ethereum could process around 30 transactions per second. While this may seem like a lot, compared to the thousands of transactions systems like Visa can handle in a second, it's minimal. With the growing popularity of dApps (decentralized applications) and ERC-20 tokens, the network has become congested, leading to delays and high transaction fees.

• SOLUTIONS ON THE HORIZON:

Ethereum is exploring several solutions to address this issue. The introduction of Ethereum 2.0, with its shift to Proof-of-Stake (PoS) and the implementation of shard chains, aims to increase the number of transactions the network can handle simultaneously.

Security: Ensuring Trust in a Decentralized World

THE IMPORTANCE OF SECURITY:

A decentralized network like Ethereum must be secure to inspire trust. Hackers are constantly searching for vulnerabilities, and a security breach could result in the loss of billions of dollars.

CHALLENGES FACED:

Events such as the DAO incident, where a vulnerability in a smart contract led to the loss of millions of dollars, underscore the importance of security on Ethereum. The complexity of smart contracts means that a single mistake can have catastrophic consequences.

STRENGTHENING THE FORTRESS:

Ethereum is continually working on improving its security. Smart contract audits, bug bounty programs, and ongoing research into network security are some of the measures in place.

Upgrades: Evolving While Maintaining Network Consistency

WHY UPGRADES ARE ESSENTIAL:

Like any technology, Ethereum must evolve to meet the changing needs of its community and incorporate new technological advancements.

CHALLENGES OF UPDATES:

Implementing an upgrade on a decentralized blockchain is not as straightforward as updating conventional software. Each upgrade requires consensus within the community. If consensus is not reached, it can lead to a «fork,» creating two distinct chains, as was the case with Ethereum and Ethereum Classic.

TOWARD A MORE FLEXIBLE FUTURE:

Ethereum is striving to implement seamless upgrades. Ethereum 2.0 is a major example, although its implementation is phased to ensure a smooth transition.

Conclusion:

Ethereum is at the forefront of blockchain technology, but this leadership comes with its share of challenges. By understanding these challenges and continually working to overcome them, Ethereum aspires not only to remain relevant but also to shape the future of decentralized finance and the decentralized internet.

4

Smart Contracts and DApps

WHAT IS A SMART CONTRACT?

Introduction:

In the complex world of blockchain, technical terms can often seem enigmatic. One such term that consistently comes up is the «Smart Contract.» But what exactly is a Smart Contract? Let's delve into this concept, from its fundamental idea to its concrete applications.

The Vending Machine Metaphor:

Imagine a vending machine for beverages. You insert a coin, select your drink, and the machine dispenses it to you. Here, there's a simple rule: if you pay the right amount and choose an available drink, the machine executes the desired action. No one needs to manually check your coin or hand you the drink. It's automatic; it's triggered by your action. A Smart Contract operates on the same principle but in the digital world of the blockchain.

Simplified Definition:

A Smart Contract is a self-executing program with instructions inscribed, verified, and executed on the blockchain. Just like the vending machine «knows» which product to dispense based on the inserted money and button pressed, the Smart Contract «knows» how to act based on the information it receives.

Origins of the Concept:

Long before Ethereum's creation, the idea of Smart Contracts was conceptualized by Nick Szabo in 1994. However, it was with the advent of Ethereum, created by Vitalik Buterin, that the true potential of Smart Contracts could be fully explored.

How It Works:

CODING AND DEPLOYMENT: It all starts with creating the Smart Contract. Developers code it to execute certain actions when specific conditions are met.

VERIFICATION: Once deployed on the blockchain, the Smart Contract is verified by network nodes. This ensures it's safe and does what it's supposed to.

EXECUTION: As soon as the conditions defined in the contract are met, it self-executes, without external intervention.

Concrete Example:

Let's take the example of an apartment rental. Instead of going through an agency, the owner and the tenant can set up a Smart Contract. If the tenant sends the agreed-upon amount, the Smart Contract could automatically provide them with a digital code to enter the apartment. At the end of the rental agreement, access would be automatically revoked. All of this happens without intermediaries, in a transparent and secure manner.

Advantages of Smart Contracts:

SECURITY: Smart Contracts are cryptographically secure and immutable. Once deployed, they cannot be altered.
TRANSPARENCY: The conditions of the Smart Contract are visible to all parties involved.
AUTOMATION: They eliminate the need for intermediaries, reducing costs and delays.
RELIABILITY: Once conditions are met, the Smart Contract will always execute as intended.

Challenges and Concerns:

However, it's worth noting that while powerful, Smart Contracts are not without challenges. Their immutability means that once an error is written, it cannot be corrected. Additionally, they require a high level of coding expertise to avoid potential vulnerabilities.

Conclusion:

Smart Contracts are one of the most revolutionary innovations brought by blockchain technology. They have the potential to radically change how we make agreements, conduct business, and interact with each other in a digital space. However, like any technology, they should be approached with a clear understanding of their benefits and limitations.

DEVELOPING ON ETHEREUM: SOLIDITY AND ASSOCIATED TOOLS

Introduction:

In the bustling universe of blockchain, Ethereum stands out as the premier platform for decentralized application development. At the core of this success lies the programming language Solidity and a suite of tools that facilitate the design, deployment, and management of Smart Contracts. But what is Solidity, and what are these essential tools? Let's embark on a journey to uncover the behind-the-scenes of Ethereum.

Solidity: The Language of the Ethereum Blockchain

DEFINITION: Solidity is a programming language specifically designed for writing Smart Contracts on Ethereum. It is to Ethereum what JavaScript is to web development: indispensable.

FEATURES: It is an object-oriented, strongly typed language with similarities to JavaScript in terms of syntax, making it relatively accessible for developers already familiar with modern programming languages.

Tools for Ethereum Development

REMIX: This is an online Integrated Development Environment (IDE) for Solidity. Remix is perfect for those new to Solidity, offering a user-friendly interface for writing, testing, and deploying smart contracts.

TRUFFLE SUITE: A popular development framework for Ethereum that includes a set of tools to ease Smart Contract development. It integrates a package management system, automated testing environment, and features for deployment and migrations.

GANACHE: Part of the Truffle Suite, Ganache is a personal Ethereum blockchain simulator. It allows developers to deploy contracts, develop applications, and run tests in a safe and controlled environment.

METAMASK: It's not just a cryptocurrency wallet. MetaMask also serves as a bridge that enables web browsers to interact with the Ethereum blockchain, making it possible to use decentralized applications directly in your browser.

The Importance of Security

When developing Smart Contracts, a strong focus on security is crucial. Due to their immutable nature and the importance of the assets they can manage, an error in a Smart Contract can have disastrous consequences. Various tools and practices, such as contract audits and rigorous testing, are essential to ensure the safety of contracts.

The Future of Ethereum Development

With technology constantly evolving and Ethereum 2.0 on the horizon, the tools and languages associated with Ethereum will also continue to evolve. The Ethereum community is active, with many developers contributing to the creation of new tools, frameworks, and improvements to facilitate development on the platform.

Conclusion:

Development on Ethereum offers a world of opportunities to create revolutionary decentralized applications. With Solidity as the cornerstone and a range of tools designed to streamline the process, developers have everything they need to unleash their creativity. However, it is essential to stay informed about best practices, technological updates, and security implications to ensure the success of any Ethereum-based project.

DAPPS (DECENTRALIZED APPLICATIONS) : EXAMPLES AND USE CASES

Introduction:

Imagine a world where applications are not owned or controlled by large corporations but rather reside in the hands of their users. Welcome to the realm of DApps, or decentralized applications. These applications, built on blockchains like Ethereum, promise to democratize the digital landscape. Let's delve into the fascinating world of DApps.

What Is a DApp?

Definition:

A decentralized application (DApp) is an application that operates on a blockchain network. Unlike traditional applications that run on centralized servers, DApps leverage the blockchain to ensure transparency, security, and resistance to censorship.

Key Characteristics:

DECENTRALIZATION: DApps are backed by a distributed network of nodes.
CONSENSUS PROTOCOL: Every change or transaction is confirmed through consensus.
OPEN SOURCE: The source code of DApps is typically accessible to the public.
TOKENS: DApps often use tokens or cryptocurrencies for internal operations.

Why Are DApps Important?

They represent a departure from the centralized model, offering increased transparency and reducing single points of failure. Moreover, they can operate without interruption, are censorship-resistant, and, in many cases, are less likely to be manipulated or controlled by a central entity.

Notable Examples of DApps:

DEFI (DECENTRALIZED FINANCE): DeFi DApps aim to replicate traditional financial services like lending, borrowing, and trading but in a decentralized manner. Example: Compound, which allows users to borrow or lend crypto assets.
GAMING: Blockchain-based games often use tokens and NFTs (non-fungible tokens) to represent in-game items. Example: CryptoKitties, a virtual cat collecting game.
NFT MARKETPLACES: These platforms facilitate the buying, selling, and trading of non-fungible tokens, which can represent art, collectibles, and more. Example: OpenSea.
DECENTRALIZED SOCIAL NETWORKS: These platforms offer an alternative to social media giants, putting data ownership in the hands of users. Example: Peepeth.

Challenges of DApps:

While they offer many advantages, DApps are not without challenges. Scalability, high transaction fees at certain times, mainstream adoption, and technological complexity are issues that developers must address.

The Future of DApps:

With the evolution of blockchain technology, especially initiatives like Ethereum 2.0, we can expect DApps to become faster, more efficient, and more accessible. As more people recognize the benefits of decentralization, we are likely to see increasing adoption of DApps across various sectors.

Conclusion:

Decentralized applications offer an alternative vision of the digital world, one where power is distributed, and users have a say in how the platforms they use operate. From finance to art, games to social networks, DApps are redefining what it means to interact online. As technology continues to mature, the future of DApps looks promising, opening the door to a more equitable and transparent digital world.

5

Decentralized Finance (DeFi) on Ethereum

INTRODUCTION TO DEFI

What Is DeFi?

Decentralized finance, often referred to as DeFi, is a term that encompasses a range of blockchain-based financial innovations aimed at replicating, transforming, and enhancing traditional financial services. Imagine a bank, an exchange, or an insurance company without intermediaries, without bureaucracy, and entirely automated. This is what DeFi promises.

The Origin of DeFi:

The rise of DeFi has its roots in the very philosophy of blockchain: decentralization. Why entrust our finances to centralized institutions, often slow and costly, when we can create transparent, fast, and intermediary-free financial systems? Ethereum, with its smart contracts, paved the way for this revolution, enabling the creation of automated and transparent financial applications.

The Key Pillars of DeFi:

ACCESSIBILITY: DeFi offers financial services without the need for a traditional bank account. All you need is a smartphone and an internet connection.

TRANSPARENCY: All transactions are recorded on a public blockchain, ensuring complete transparency.

CONTROL AND OWNERSHIP: Users have full control over their funds without intermediaries.

PROGRAMMABILITY: DeFi services can be automated and interconnected through the use of smart contracts.

Examples of DeFi Services:

LENDING AND BORROWING: Platforms like Compound and Aave allow users to lend and borrow cryptocurrencies without the need for a financial institution.

DECENTRALIZED EXCHANGES (DEXS): Unlike traditional exchanges, DEXs like Uniswap or Sushiswap enable direct cryptocurrency trading without intermediaries.

DECENTRALIZED INSURANCE: Projects like Nexus Mutual offer blockchain-based insurance coverage, protecting against various risks in the crypto ecosystem.

STABLECOINS: These are cryptocurrencies pegged to a fiat currency like the US dollar. USDC and DAI are popular examples.

Challenges and Considerations:

DeFi, while innovative, is not without risks. Concerns include faulty smart contracts, liquidity risks, and security vulnerabilities. Moreover, the complexity of DeFi products can often be confusing for new users.

Conclusion:

Decentralized finance represents a major revolution in the financial world. It challenges traditional methods and offers more transparent, efficient, and accessible alternatives. However, like any innovation, it comes with challenges and risks. With the right balance of regulation, education, and innovation, DeFi has the potential to redefine how we understand and interact with finance.

LEADING DEFI PROJECTS ON ETHEREUM: UNISWAP, COMPOUND, MAKERDAO, AND MORE

Background: The Emergence of DeFi Projects on Ethereum

Ethereum, as a platform for decentralized applications (DApps) and smart contracts, laid the foundation for the decentralized finance (DeFi) revolution. This rapidly growing ecosystem has seen numerous ambitious projects emerge, each with its own vision to rethink and disrupt various segments of the traditional financial sector. Let's take a closer look at some of the most iconic DeFi projects on Ethereum.

Uniswap: The Definitive Decentralized Exchange

OVERVIEW: Uniswap is a decentralized exchange (DEX) protocol on Ethereum. Unlike centralized exchanges like Binance or Coinbase, Uniswap enables users to swap tokens directly with one another, without intermediaries.

INNOVATION: Its unique mechanism, based on «liquidity pools,» allows users to provide funds to ensure liquidity and earn fees in return. Token prices are determined by an algorithm based on the token balance in the pool.

IMPACT: Uniswap has radically simplified token trading on Ethereum, becoming one of the most popular and widely used DEXs.

Compound: Revolutionizing Lending and Borrowing

OVERVIEW: Compound is a DeFi protocol that enables users to lend and borrow cryptocurrencies in a decentralized manner.

INNOVATION: Users supply their tokens as collateral to borrow other tokens. Interest rates are algorithmically determined based on supply and demand.

IMPACT: Compound has paved the way for a new form of decentralized money market where users can earn interest on their assets or borrow other assets as needed.

MakerDAO and DAI: The Birth of Decentralized Stablecoin

OVERVIEW: MakerDAO is a DeFi protocol that enables the creation of DAI, a stablecoin closely pegged to the US dollar. However, unlike other stablecoins, DAI is not backed by real-dollar reserves but rather supported by other assets on the Ethereum blockchain.

INNOVATION: Users lock their assets (like ETH) into the Maker protocol to generate DAI. This process ensures that each DAI is always backed by a higher value in assets, stabilizing its value.

IMPACT: DAI has become one of the most popular decentralized stablecoins, offering stability in the often volatile world of cryptocurrencies.

Other Notable Projects:

AAVE: A lending platform that introduced innovative features like «Flash Loans.»

YEARN.FINANCE: Aims to simplify DeFi for the average user by automating yield maximization.

CURVE FINANCE: An exchange for stablecoin-to-stablecoin trading, optimizing to offer users the best rates.

Conclusion: The DeFi ecosystem on Ethereum is rich and diverse, offering solutions for nearly every challenge posed by the traditional financial system. These projects, while technically complex, share a common mission to make finance more open, accessible, and equitable for all. As the ecosystem continues to evolve, it will be exciting to see how these projects and others transform the way we interact with money in the future.

CHALLENGES AND ISSUES IN DEFI

Introduction: The Emergence of DeFi

Decentralized finance, commonly known as DeFi, represents a radical transformation of the financial landscape. By utilizing blockchain technology, particularly Ethereum, it aims to democratize financial services, making them accessible to everyone without intermediaries. However, like any innovation, DeFi faces a set of challenges and significant issues.

The Significance of DeFi: Why It Matters

FINANCIAL INCLUSION: DeFi has the potential to offer financial services to billions of unbanked people worldwide, providing them with means to save, borrow, and invest.

TRANSPARENCY: Everything is coded and verifiable on the blockchain, meaning that unlike traditional financial institutions, users can see exactly how protocols operate.

MINIMAL INTERMEDIATION: By eliminating intermediaries, users can often obtain better rates and avoid excessive fees.

Technical Challenges: Ensuring Security and Efficiency

SECURITY VULNERABILITIES: Since DeFi relies on software, it is susceptible to bugs and vulnerabilities. Attacks like the one on the bZx protocol have highlighted associated risks.

SCALABILITY: Congested networks, especially Ethereum, can result in high transaction fees, making some DeFi applications costly to use.

INTEROPERABILITY: As DeFi spans multiple blockchains, it is crucial for these different platforms to interact seamlessly.

Regulatory Challenges: Navigating an Unregulated World

LACK OF REGULATION: DeFi evolves faster than regulators can keep up. The absence of clear regulations can lead to misuse or fraudulent activities.

LEGAL RISKS: Without clear legal frameworks, those launching or investing in DeFi projects may face unforeseen legal risks.

Other Concerns: Economics and Centralization

ECONOMIC RISKS: The volatility of cryptocurrencies and underlying assets can impact the stability of DeFi protocols, leading to liquidity crises or «bank runs.»

CENTRALIZATION RISK: Some DeFi protocols, despite claiming decentralization, retain centralized control mechanisms, potentially challenging the essence of DeFi.

EDUCATION AND ADOPTION: The complexity and technical nature of DeFi can deter mass adoption. Adequate education is essential to prevent users from making costly mistakes.

Conclusion:

DeFi stands at a crossroads. Its revolutionary potential is undeniable, but the challenges it faces are substantial. For DeFi to fully realize its vision of open and equitable finance, developers, users, and regulators must collaborate to overcome these obstacles. The future of finance may well depend on how these challenges are addressed.

6

ERC-20, ERC-721, and Other Token Standards

INTRODUCTION TO TOKENS AND THEIR UTILITY

Tokens in the world of blockchain are digital representations of an asset or right. Think of them like tokens at an amusement park that can be exchanged for a ride or service. In the blockchain, these tokens can represent a myriad of things, from company stocks to gold, customer loyalty, and even digital artworks.

Utility of Tokens:

ASSET REPRESENTATION: Tokens can represent real-world assets like gold or real estate, enabling smoother transactions and exchanges.

MEDIUM OF EXCHANGE: In some blockchain ecosystems, tokens serve as currency to purchase services or goods.

GOVERNANCE: Some tokens allow their holders to vote on decisions concerning a project's direction.

ACCESS: Certain services require tokens to function, similar to a key.

ERC-20: The Standard for Fungible Tokens

ERC-20 is a set of rules (or protocol) that tokens on Ethereum must adhere to in order to be interoperable with other products or services. These are «fungible» tokens, meaning each token is identical and has the same value as other tokens.

Why Is ERC-20 So Important?

INTERCHANGEABILITY: ERC-20 compliance ensures these tokens can be exchanged or used in any wallet, exchange, or service that recognizes this standard.

SIMPLICITY: For developers, creating a new token based on this standard is relatively straightforward and ensures broad acceptance.

ERC-721: The Rise of Non-Fungible Tokens (NFTs)

Unlike ERC-20, ERC-721 is a standard for tokens that are not interchangeable, meaning non-fungible tokens (NFTs). Each NFT is distinct and may have a different value from other tokens.

Why Are NFTs Revolutionary?

UNIQUENESS: They often represent unique digital assets like artworks, sports memorabilia, or even virtual lands.
PROOF OF OWNERSHIP: On the blockchain, ownership of an NFT is indisputable. If you own an NFT representing a digital artwork, it's akin to having a certificate of authenticity.
DYNAMIC MARKET: NFTs have opened up a new market for artists, creators, and collectors.

Other Standards and Their Significance

There are several other token standards on Ethereum, each serving its own purpose:

ERC-1155: A standard that can create both fungible and non-fungible tokens. It is particularly popular in video games to represent items like weapons or costumes.
ERC-1337: This standard is for recurring subscriptions on Ethereum, enabling periodic payments.
Each standard addresses a specific need within the community, enabling a range of possibilities and applications that were not possible in traditional financial systems.

Conclusion

In the Ethereum ecosystem, tokens play a vital role in representing a wide range of assets and rights. Through standards like ERC-20 and ERC-721, Ethereum has opened the door to a revolution in how we perceive ownership, exchange, and value in the digital world. These tokens, though still young, have the potential to transform many sectors, from finance to art, gaming, and beyond.

7

Ethereum in the Global Blockchain Landscape

ETHEREUM VS. BITCOIN: COMPARISON AND SYNERGY

Introduction

Ethereum and Bitcoin, the giants of the cryptocurrency world, are often compared and sometimes, albeit mistakenly, considered competitors. While they may seem similar at first glance, as they both utilize blockchain technology, their objectives, uses, and underlying mechanisms differ significantly. Let's explore these differences while highlighting how they can work in synergy.

Birth and Objectives

Bitcoin, launched in 2009 by an anonymous entity known as Satoshi Nakamoto, was designed as a peer-to-peer electronic currency, providing a solution to the double-spending problem without the need for a central authority. Its primary goal was to create a decentralized, censorship-resistant currency with a limited supply (21 million bitcoins max).

Ethereum, proposed in 2013 by Vitalik Buterin and launched in 2015, has broader ambitions. Beyond being just a currency, Ethereum aims to be a platform for creating smart contracts and decentralized applications. Its goal is to decentralize the Internet and empower developers to build applications on its platform.

Underlying Technology

Both projects operate on blockchain technology, but their blockchains are inherently different.
Bitcoin has a blockchain primarily designed to handle monetary transactions. It is simpler, secure, and optimized for storing and verifying bitcoin movements.
Ethereum, on the other hand, has a blockchain that serves as a global computer. It can process not only transactions but also complex code for smart contracts and DApps. This flexibility comes with some complexity and challenges, such as scalability.

Scripting Language

Bitcoin has a scripting language, but it is relatively limited in terms of functionalities. It is designed to handle basic transactions, such as multi-signature. Ethereum uses «Solidity,» a programming language that allows developers to write complex smart contracts. It offers great flexibility but also increased complexity and requires special attention to security.

Token Economics

Bitcoin has only one type of token, Bitcoin (BTC), used both as a currency and to reward miners.
Ethereum has Ether (ETH) as its primary currency, but its platform also hosts countless other tokens created through smart contracts, such as ERC-20 tokens.

Synergies

While often compared as rivals, Bitcoin and Ethereum have different objectives and can coexist harmoniously.
STORE OF VALUE VS. FUEL FOR APPLICATIONS: Bitcoin is often seen as «digital gold,» a store of value, while Ethereum is the fuel needed to run applications on its platform.
INTEROPERABILITY: Many projects seek to connect these two blockchains to benefit from Bitcoin's security and Ethereum's flexibility.
ADOPTION: Bitcoin's popularity has paved the way for cryptocurrency acceptance, indirectly benefiting Ethereum.

Conclusion

Ethereum and Bitcoin, though often juxtaposed, are pillars of the cryptocurrency world with distinct visions. One seeks to revolutionize currency as we know it, while the other aspires to a decentralized Internet. Understanding their differences is crucial, but it is equally essential to see how they can complement each other in the broader blockchain ecosystem.

OTHER SMART CONTRACT PLATFORMS AND THE FUTURE OF ETHEREUM IN THE MARKET

AWhile Ethereum has been a pioneer in the realm of smart contracts and decentralized applications, several other platforms have emerged, aiming to address some of the challenges faced by Ethereum or offer innovative solutions. Among these platforms, EOS, Tron, and Cardano stand out. Understanding these alternatives, as well as Ethereum's position in the evolving market, is essential for gaining a comprehensive view of the cryptocurrency ecosystem.

EOS: The Performance-Oriented Blockchain

EOS is often referred to as the «Ethereum Killer» due to its ambition to outperform Ethereum in terms of performance and scalability.
Delegated Proof-of-Stake: EOS employs a consensus model called Delegated Proof-of-Stake (DPoS). This means that only a few nodes, selected by the community, are responsible for validating transactions, making the process faster.
Transaction Fees: Another feature of EOS is the absence of transaction fees for end-users. However, developers must «stake» (lock up) a certain amount of EOS to ensure the power and bandwidth needed for their applications to run.

Tron: Focused on Digital Content

Tron aims to build a decentralized platform for content sharing, where creators can be directly rewarded for their work.
Acquisition of BitTorrent: As part of its strategy, Tron acquired BitTorrent, one of the largest peer-to-peer file-sharing platforms. This could pave the way for deep blockchain integration into large-scale content sharing.
Performance: Like EOS, Tron also utilizes a DPoS consensus model to offer high transaction speeds.

Cardano: An Academic Approach

Cardano distinguishes itself through a methodical approach based on academic research and peer review.

Layered Structure: Cardano has a layered structure, separating the settlement layer (where transactions occur) from the computation layer (where smart contracts execute). This separation aims to enhance network flexibility and scalability.

Sustainable Development: One of Cardano's goals is to create a sustainable, interoperable, and scalable blockchain platform.

THE FUTURE OF THE MARKET AND ETHEREUM'S POSITION

As the world becomes increasingly aware of the need to protect our planet, the environmental impact of emerging technologies like blockchain is becoming a hot topic of discussion. Cryptocurrencies, despite their many promises, are often criticized for their carbon footprint. In this context, how does Ethereum, one of the market leaders, position itself, and how do its choices influence the future of the sector?

The Current Environmental Context

RISING ENVIRONMENTAL AWARENESS: Globally, citizens, businesses, and governments are becoming more aware of the need for environmental action. Climate agreements like the Paris Agreement reflect this shared commitment to a more sustainable future.

TECHNOLOGIES UNDER SCRUTINY: In this context, all industries are scrutinized, including the tech sector. Data centers, electronic component manufacturing processes, and now cryptocurrencies are all under the spotlight.

The Cryptocurrency Market and Ecology

ENERGY CONSUMPTION: Proof-of-Work, the underlying mechanism for many cryptocurrencies, including Bitcoin, is particularly energy-intensive. It requires a phenomenal amount of computational power, leading to electricity consumption comparable to that of small countries.

ECO-FRIENDLY ALTERNATIVES: Some cryptocurrencies seek to differentiate themselves by adopting less energy-intensive mechanisms or by offsetting their carbon footprint. However, these initiatives remain minority practices for now.

Ethereum at a Crossroads

A LEADER AWARE OF ITS FOOTPRINT: Ethereum, due to its market weight, is under close scrutiny. Its energy consumption, while lower than that of Bitcoin, is significant.

TRANSITION TO ETHEREUM 2.0: Recognizing these challenges, the Ethereum ecosystem has initiated a transition to Ethereum 2.0, based on Proof-of-Stake. This mechanism, far less energy-intensive, signals Ethereum's intent to position itself as a next-generation, environmentally friendly blockchain.

IMPACT ON THE MARKET: Ethereum's approach could potentially set an example for other blockchain projects, encouraging an overall reduction in the sector's carbon footprint.

Conclusion

As environmental pressure intensifies, the cryptocurrency market, particularly Ethereum, stands at a crossroads. The choices made today will shape the perception and acceptance of these technologies tomorrow. Through its initiatives towards a greener blockchain, Ethereum could not only solidify its leadership position but also contribute to steering the entire industry towards a more sustainable future.

8

Challenges and Controversies

ETHEREUM AND ITS CHALLENGES: ENERGY CONSUMPTION, SCALABILITY, AND SECURITY

ENVIRONMENTAL CONCERNS: ENERGY CONSUMPTION

In the current era of heightened awareness about climate change and sustainability, blockchain technology, particularly Ethereum, has become a focal point due to its significant energy requirements. This text aims to break down the nature of this energy consumption, why it matters, and the measures taken to address it.

PROOF OF WORK: ENERGY-INTENSIVE

Ethereum, like Bitcoin, initially adopted a consensus mechanism called Proof of Work (PoW). This system requires miners to solve complex cryptographic puzzles to add a new block to the blockchain. This process is competitive, meaning miners worldwide are constantly racing to solve the puzzle as quickly as possible.

POW IS INHERENTLY ENERGY-INTENSIVE FOR SEVERAL REASONS:

COMPETITION OVER COOPERATION: In PoW, all miners work on the same puzzle, but only one of them will win the right to add the next block. This means that most of the energy expended is wasted.

SPECIALIZED HARDWARE: To maximize their chances, miners use highly specialized hardware, often called ASICs, designed to solve these puzzles as quickly as possible. These devices consume a significant amount of electricity.

ENVIRONMENTAL IMPLICATIONS

The massive energy consumption of Ethereum raises major concerns, such as:

CARBON EMISSIONS: If the energy used comes from non-renewable sources, it contributes significantly to carbon emissions, exacerbating climate change challenges.

STRAIN ON ENERGY INFRASTRUCTURE: Mining farms can put enormous pressure on local electrical grids, especially in regions where the infrastructure is not equipped to handle such demand.

MEASURES TOWARD A GREENER SOLUTION
Faced with these challenges, the Ethereum community has taken active steps to reduce its carbon footprint:

TRANSITION TO PROOF OF STAKE (POS): Ethereum 2.0 aims to replace PoW with Proof of Stake (PoS), a much less energy-intensive mechanism. In PoS, block creation is based on ownership of currency rather than the ability to solve cryptographic puzzles.

EXPERIMENTATION WITH LAYER 2 SOLUTIONS: These solutions, like Rollups, allow transactions to occur off the main blockchain, reducing the load on the main network.

ADOPTION OF RENEWABLE ENERGY: Some miners commit to using only renewable energy to power their operations, although implementation varies by region and incentives.

CONCLUSION
Ethereum's energy consumption is a legitimate concern, especially in an era where sustainability and environmental conservation are of utmost importance. Fortunately, with the advent of Ethereum 2.0 and other innovations, the blockchain is on the path to becoming much more environmentally friendly while retaining its revolutionary benefits.

SCALABILITY ISSUES AND PROPOSED SOLUTIONS

The term «scalability» refers to a system's ability to handle an increase in workload or demand while maintaining its performance. In the world of blockchain, especially for Ethereum, scalability is a central concern. This challenge, critical for the development and widespread adoption of this technology, requires an understanding of its causes, implications, and proposed solutions.

Origin of the Problem

BLOCKCHAIN NATURE: By design, every transaction on Ethereum must be verified by the entire network, ensuring security and decentralization but limiting the speed at which transactions can be processed.

GROWING NETWORK SIZE: With the increasing number of users and decentralized applications (DApps) on Ethereum, the number of transactions to be processed simultaneously has surged.

Implications of Scalability

HIGH TRANSACTION FEES: When the network is congested, users are often forced to increase the fees (or «gas») they are willing to pay for their transactions to be prioritized.

TRANSACTION DELAYS: During peak activity, transactions can take much longer than expected to be confirmed.

ADOPTION HURDLES: These issues can discourage new users or businesses from adopting Ethereum for their needs, limiting its potential.

Proposed Solutions

ETHEREUM 2.0: This is a major network upgrade that aims to replace the current consensus mechanism (Proof of Work) with Proof of Stake. This transition should greatly improve Ethereum's ability to process a higher number of transactions per second.

LAYER 2 SOLUTIONS: These technologies, such as Rollups and state channels, allow much of the processing to occur off the main blockchain before consolidating results on it. This speeds up transactions while minimizing the load on the main blockchain.

SHARDING: Proposed as part of Ethereum 2.0, sharding divides the blockchain into multiple «shards» that can process transactions simultaneously.

SIDECHAINS: These are separate blockchains that run in parallel with Ethereum and are designed to offload a portion of the transaction volume.

Conclusion

Scalability is one of the most pressing challenges Ethereum faces today. The explosive growth of DeFi, NFTs, and other innovative applications on Ethereum has exacerbated these issues. However, the Ethereum community and developers are fully aware of these challenges and actively working to implement solutions. With the expected adoption of Ethereum 2.0 and other technological improvements, Ethereum's future as a scalable and usable platform appears promising.améliorations technologiques, l'avenir d'Ethereum en tant que plateforme évolutive et utilisable semble prometteur.

SECURITY ON ETHEREUM: FRAUDS, HACKS, AND LESSONS LEARNED

At the heart of the technological and economic excitement that Ethereum embodies lie two major concerns for its users and the general public: its environmental impact and security. While the potential offered by Ethereum and its blockchain is immense, it is not without consequences or risks.

Ethereum's Environmental Impact

PROOF OF WORK (POW) ENERGY CONSUMPTION: Historically, Ethereum, like Bitcoin, relies on the Proof of Work mechanism to validate transactions. This process is extremely energy-intensive, as it requires significant computational power used by miners to solve cryptographic puzzles.

COMPARISONS TO ENTIRE COUNTRIES: According to some estimates, the Ethereum network consumes as much energy as some countries. These, at times, alarming figures are at the center of many discussions regarding the environmental viability of cryptocurrencies.

TRANSITION TO PROOF OF STAKE (POS): In response to these concerns, Ethereum 2.0 is moving toward a Proof of Stake model, which is much less energy-intensive. It represents a significant step toward a more environmentally friendly Ethereum.

Security on Ethereum

DECENTRALIZED NATURE AND ASSOCIATED RISKS: Ethereum's open and decentralized architecture, while its strength, also makes it vulnerable to various types of attacks.

MAJOR HACKS:

THE DAO: In 2016, a vulnerability in the DAO (Decentralized Autonomous Organization) code allowed an individual to siphon off a large amount of Ether, leading to a controversial fork of the Ethereum blockchain.

PARITY: A flaw in Parity's multi-signature wallet resulted in the loss of hundreds of thousands of ETH.

Lessons Learned:

PRIORITIZING SECURITY: Major incidents have pushed developers to prioritize security. Contract audits have become commonplace, and the community is increasingly vigilant.

EVOLVING PRACTICES: The Ethereum community has adopted stricter standards for smart contract development, particularly regarding error handling and upgrade mechanisms.

Conclusion

Ethereum, like any innovative technology, operates in a delicate balance between the promise of revolution and unprecedented challenges. Environmental and security concerns are not to be taken lightly, but the Ethereum community's ability to adapt and innovate in the face.

9

The Future of Ethereum

ETHEREUM 2.0, THE ERA OF DEFI, AND THE VISION FOR THE FUTURE

Ethereum 2.0 and the Transition to Proof-of-Stake

If Ethereum is often compared to a superhighway of information, then Ethereum 2.0 might well be considered the shift from a two-lane road to a vast interconnected network of highways. The core of this transformation lies in the fundamental change of its consensus mechanism: the transition from Proof-of-Work (PoW) to Proof-of-Stake (PoS). But what does this truly mean, and why is it so revolutionary?

The Challenge of Proof-of-Work

Ethereum, like Bitcoin, originally operated on a PoW consensus mechanism. In PoW, miners use immense computational power to solve cryptographic puzzles, and the first to find the solution adds a new block to the blockchain. While this mechanism is secure, it presents two major challenges:

ENERGY CONSUMPTION: The competition among miners to solve these puzzles consumes an astronomical amount of energy, raising environmental concerns.

SCALABILITY: PoW has its limits in terms of speed and the volume of transactions it can handle, limiting Ethereum's capacity for broader usage.

The Light at the End of the Tunnel: Proof-of-Stake

Proof-of-Stake radically changes how new blocks are created and validated on the blockchain. Instead of relying on raw computational power, PoS is based on the amount of cryptocurrency an individual holds and is willing to «stake» or «lock up» as collateral. In simplified terms:

1. Participants who wish to validate transactions and create new blocks lock up a certain amount of Ether as collateral.

2. These validators are then randomly selected to propose and validate new blocks, based on the amount of Ether they have staked, among other factors.

3. If a validator acts dishonestly, they lose a portion or all of their stake. If, on the other hand, they act honestly, they receive rewards in the form of Ether.

The Advantages of Ethereum 2.0 and PoS

ENERGY EFFICIENCY: The absence of competition based on computational power makes PoS a much greener alternative to PoW. This means reduced carbon footprint and a more environmentally friendly network.

ENHANCED SECURITY: With validators staking their own funds, there is a strong economic incentive to act honestly.

IMPROVED SCALABILITY: Ethereum 2.0, along with other mechanisms like sharding, can process many more transactions per second than its previous version.

The Transition Phases

The transition to Ethereum 2.0 is a multi-stage process, including Phase 0 (launch of the beacon chain and introduction of PoS), Phase 1 (introduction of sharding), and Phase 2 (full integration with the Ethereum we know today).

Conclusion

Ethereum 2.0 and Proof-of-Stake mark a new era for Ethereum's blockchain. By addressing key challenges of scalability and energy consumption, this upgrade opens the door to a future where Ethereum could become the backbone of many financial and non-financial systems worldwide. The transition to this new era is a testament to Ethereum's ongoing evolution and its quest to fulfill its original vision.

THE EXPECTED EVOLUTION OF DAPPS AND DEFI

Introduction

Decentralized applications (DApps) and decentralized finance (DeFi) are two of the most remarkable achievements in the Ethereum ecosystem. As Ethereum continues to grow, it's crucial to understand how these innovations are evolving and what the future may hold for them.

Understanding DApps

DApps are applications that run on a blockchain rather than centralized servers. Thanks to this architecture, they inherit intrinsic blockchain properties such as transparency, security, and resistance to censorship.

The Evolution of DApps

DIVERSIFICATION OF DOMAINS: While early DApps primarily focused on gaming and exchanges, we now see DApps in areas such as healthcare, education, logistics, and more.

IMPROVED USER INTERFACE: Early DApps were often criticized for their lack of user-friendliness. However, newer generations of DApps focus more on the user experience, making blockchain usage more accessible to the general public.

INCREASED INTERCONNECTIVITY: DApps are starting to interact with each other, creating an interconnected ecosystem where users can seamlessly move from one application to another.

Understanding DeFi

DeFi (Decentralized Finance) aims to create an open and permissionless financial system using blockchain technology. It offers services such as lending, borrowing, trading, insurance, and more, without the need for intermediaries like banks.

The Evolution of DeFi

GROWING COMPLEXITY: Early DeFi products were simple, but over time, they have become increasingly complex, offering a range of sophisticated financial services.

DECENTRALIZED GOVERNANCE: Many DeFi projects implement governance mechanisms that allow users to vote and make decisions regarding the project's future development.

INTEROPERABILITY: As the DeFi ecosystem grows, interoperability between different platforms becomes crucial. Protocols like «wrapped tokens» and bridges between blockchains enable the integration of various assets into the Ethereum DeFi ecosystem.

The Future of DApps and DeFi

MASS ADOPTION: With more user-friendly interfaces and increased awareness, we are likely to see much broader adoption of DApps and DeFi in the coming years.

REGULATION: The rapid growth of DeFi has attracted regulatory attention. While this may pose challenges, thoughtful regulation could also bring greater legitimacy to the sector.

CONTINUOUS INNOVATION: With Ethereum 2.0 and other technical advancements, expect to see even more innovative DApps and DeFi solutions capable of handling larger transaction volumes and offering more sophisticated services.

Conclusion

The DApps and DeFi ecosystem on Ethereum is constantly evolving. It adapts, innovates, and overcomes challenges to realize the promise of a more open, transparent, and equitable global economy. By keeping an eye on these developments, we can better understand the transformative potential of blockchain and Ethereum for the world of tomorrow.

LONG-TERM VISION: WHAT DOES THE FUTURE HOLD FOR ETHEREUM?

Looking at the technological horizon, Ethereum stands out as a major force, not only in the world of cryptocurrencies but also in the reshaping of traditional global systems. With its constant evolution and thriving ecosystem, what future can we anticipate for Ethereum?

Mainstream Adoption

The first thing to acknowledge is that, despite its growing popularity, Ethereum is still in its infancy in terms of mainstream adoption. While DeFi and NFTs have gained significant attention, they still represent a small fraction of the global economy. In the long term, we can expect Ethereum to become more widespread, touching areas like real estate, healthcare, governance, and more. Ease of use and improved user interfaces will play a key role in this adoption.

Technological Advancement

Ethereum 2.0 marks a crucial step for the platform, but it's just the beginning. Scalability, security, and sustainability are ongoing challenges. In the long term, we may see Ethereum adopt even more advanced technological solutions, such as sharding or rollups, to increase its capacity.

Interconnection with Other Blockchains

The future of blockchains may not belong to a single dominant chain but to an interconnected network of multiple blockchains. Ethereum could act as a major hub in this interconnected ecosystem, collaborating with other blockchains to form a decentralized mesh.

A Shift Towards Sustainability

The issue of Ethereum's energy consumption is a hot topic. While the transition to Proof of Stake with Ethereum 2.0 promises a significant reduction in energy consumption, the Ethereum team could also explore even greener solutions to ensure long-term sustainability.

Socioeconomic Impacts

With its ability to democratize access to finance and other services, Ethereum could play a central role in creating a more equitable society. Decentralized finance could be a game-changer for the unbanked, and transparent voting systems could enhance participatory democracy.

Conclusion

The path of Ethereum is paved with innovation and challenges. If the past is any indication of the future, Ethereum will continue to evolve, adapt, and overcome obstacles. As a pioneer in the world of smart contracts and DeFi, its long-term vision appears promising, with the potential to profoundly transform global socioeconomic structures. While the future is inherently uncertain, one thing is clear: Ethereum will be at the center of many discussions, innovations, and transformations.

Conclusion

ETHEREUM AND THE BLOCKCHAIN REVOLUTION: PROFOUND SOCIO-ECONOMIC IMPACT

Ethereum's Place in the Blockchain Revolution

The emergence of blockchain technology has been likened to that of the internet in the 1990s in terms of revolutionary significance. At the heart of this revolution lies Ethereum, which, while often mentioned in the same breath as Bitcoin, offers much broader applications.

Where Bitcoin was primarily designed as a decentralized digital currency, Ethereum was born with a broader ambition: to serve as a platform for executing decentralized programs called «smart contracts.» These smart contracts can be likened to software applications but without the possibility of shutdown, censorship, or modification by a third party.

Ethereum amplifies the blockchain revolution by providing a canvas where ideas can be built, tested, and implemented. It's a blank slate for innovation, ranging from transparent voting systems to prediction markets and decentralized finance. In other words, Ethereum is at the heart of the disruptive potential of blockchain.

Reflections on Its Potential Socio-Economic Impact

The socio-economic potential of Ethereum is monumental. Here are some areas of impact:

DECENTRALIZED FINANCE (DEFI): Ethereum's ability to execute smart contracts has given rise to DeFi, where traditional financial services like lending, borrowing, and trading are offered without intermediaries. This could democratize access to finance, especially in underbanked regions of the world.

TRANSPARENCY AND ANTI-CORRUPTION: Ethereum-based systems make transactions transparent and immutable. This can help combat corruption by ensuring that funds reach their intended destinations.

DIGITAL IDENTITY: Ethereum-based solutions can provide secure and tamper-proof digital identities. This is crucial for refugees and other displaced populations, enabling them to access essential services and rights.

OWNERSHIP AND CREATIVITY: Ethereum's NFTs (Non-Fungible Tokens) offer artists and creators a new and innovative way to monetize their work while ensuring authenticity and provenance.

PROCESS AUTOMATION: From supply chains to real estate, smart contracts can automate, secure, and make transparent processes that were once cumbersome and error-prone.

SHARING ECONOMY: Ethereum could redefine how we share goods and services, shifting from intermediaries like Uber or Airbnb to truly peer-to-peer models.

Ultimately, Ethereum is not just a technology or a platform. It's the catalyst for a new socio-economic era, an era of transparency, inclusion, and innovation. Its potential is immense, but like any technology, its ethical use, regulation, and societal acceptance will determine its true scope and long-term impact.